Bernadette Cuxart

ART
Painting with...

BARRON'S

eNTS

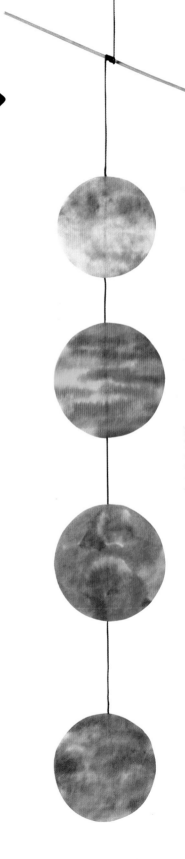

You can make drawings on a paper
without even touching it....
Do you know how?

MONSTERS with a straw

MATERIALS: Drinking straws, construction paper, dye (liquid watercolor), a painter's palette to mix the paints, brushes, googly eyes, glue, markers, and a glass of water.

1 Prepare the material that you are going to use and put the colors you want to mix on the palette. If you don't have a painter's palette, a plastic egg carton will work as well.

2 Dip the brush in the paint and drip a large drop onto the construction paper.

3 Quickly pick up the straw and blow onto the drop, so that it spreads in every direction. Do the same thing with other colors. Sometimes the paint will touch and the colors will mix, and the effect is even more fun.

4 When you have enough spots, let them dry. If you glue eyes on them and paint mouths…they will look like monsters!

It also looks good if you draw a face and use this technique to make the hair. Try it, you'll be surprised!

Painting with different colors at the same time is great, keep trying new ideas.

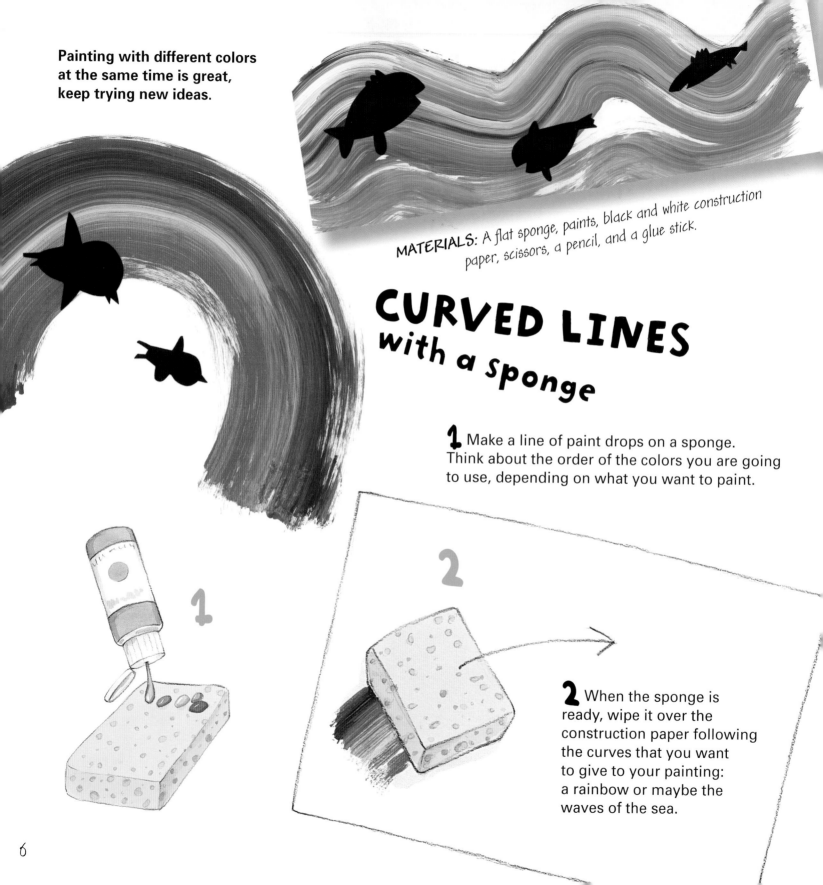

MATERIALS: A flat sponge, paints, black and white construction paper, scissors, a pencil, and a glue stick.

CURVED LINES
with a sponge

1 Make a line of paint drops on a sponge. Think about the order of the colors you are going to use, depending on what you want to paint.

1

2

2 When the sponge is ready, wipe it over the construction paper following the curves that you want to give to your painting: a rainbow or maybe the waves of the sea.

3 While the paint is drying, draw little animals on the black construction paper and cut them out. What are you making, birds or fish?

Remember that you have to clean the sponge well when you are finished, and before the paint dries.

4 Finally, glue the animals on the design you've chosen, and admire your multi-colored painting.

You don't have any paintbrushes? No problem! Your fingers are always there…

MATERIALS: Paints, plates, water, rags, construction paper, a pencil, and a marker.

PAINTING
with your fingers

1 The first thing you have to do is wash your hands well, because your fingers have to be clean if you are going to use them to paint, right? Then, pour the paints you want to use onto a plate.

2 Use the pencil to draw a picture on the construction paper and go over it again with the marker. Now you can dip your finger in the paint and begin to color in the drawing. Use different colors depending on the subject you've chosen.

3 Now try making animals using your fingertips. Do a few and think about what kind of animal each one might be.

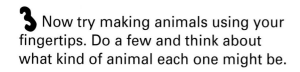

4 Use a marker to fill in the details: ears, antennae, paws, eyes…

Notice how your fingers leave different marks depending on how you use them: do you use only the tip, the whole finger....

With a paint roller you can paint very quickly. But here you are going to do much more than that…

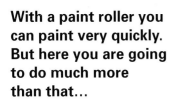

FAIRY AND STARS
with a paint roller

MATERIALS: A sponge roller, white or colored paper, acrylic paint, plastic (polystyrene) tray, thick cardboard, large scissors, tape (regular and two-sided), markers, and string or other materials.

1 Cut pieces of cardboard of the same thickness in order to make your shapes. If you want to make them thicker, you can tape together two equally-sized cut out shapes.

2 Make the figure you want and stick the pieces to the table using two-sided tape. Put a piece of paper on top so that it covers the shapes and make sure the paper doesn't move by taping it to the table.

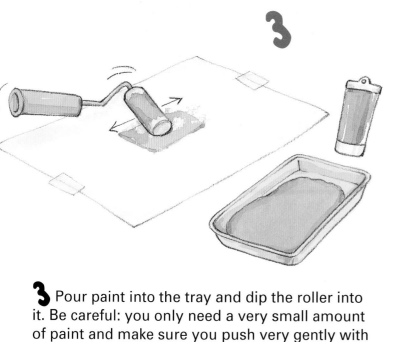

3 Pour paint into the tray and dip the roller into it. Be careful: you only need a very small amount of paint and make sure you push very gently with the roller, to make sure you don't break the paper.

4 The shapes and figures that you cut out will be clearly marked on the paper... It seems like magic! Now you are ready to remove the paper and let it dry. Later you can fill in the details with a marker.

You can also use strings, erasers, coins.... Just keep in mind that all the objects for a figure have to be the same thickness.

LANDSCAPES

Who said that you can only use paintbrushes that you buy in a store?…

with homemade brushes

1

2

MATERIALS: Paints, construction paper, scissors, glue stick, clothespins, erasers, plates, and brushes to mix the different colors and materials like feathers, sponges, string, pine needles, pieces of straw, wool, ribbons…

1 This is an exercise in making your own paintbrushes, using materials like clothespins, erasers, sticks, etc. You can get some ideas from the pictures on this page.

2 Do you have some good ideas? Now you can try them out. Use different colors of paint on a variety of colored backgrounds and try out all the brushes. Create a lot of different samples.

3 When your samples have dried, try mixing them up, and cutting them into different shapes with the scissors. For example, you could use the various parts to make up a landscape.

4 Once you have a clear idea of what you're going to make, go ahead and glue the pieces together. Work from top to bottom and glue the pieces on top of each other.

I bet you can come up with different brushstrokes... What could you make them with?

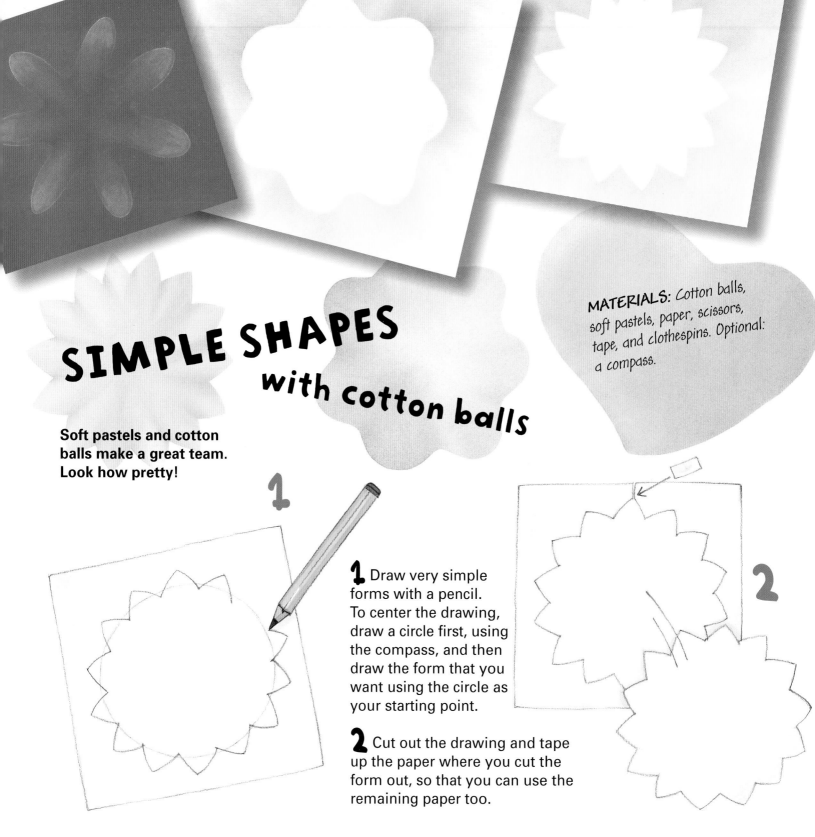

SIMPLE SHAPES
with cotton balls

Soft pastels and cotton balls make a great team. Look how pretty!

MATERIALS: Cotton balls, soft pastels, paper, scissors, tape, and clothespins. Optional: a compass.

1 Draw very simple forms with a pencil. To center the drawing, draw a circle first, using the compass, and then draw the form that you want using the circle as your starting point.

2 Cut out the drawing and tape up the paper where you cut the form out, so that you can use the remaining paper too.

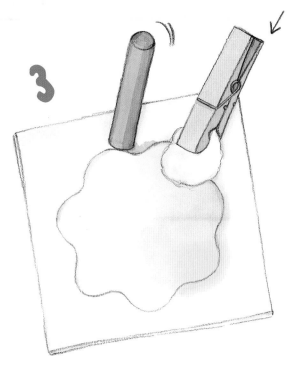

3

3 Put the leftover paper on a fresh piece of paper. Trace the cut out with soft pastels and rub the color into toward the center with a cotton ball (you can hold the cotton with your fingers or with a clothespin). Hold the papers with your free hand, so that they don't move.

4

Glue your drawings on construction paper cards and you'll have some great cards to give to your friends.

4 Now take the cut out and center it on another piece of paper. Color the borders with the soft pastels and spread them outward using cotton balls. Now you have a white flower on a colored background. Which one do you like more?

A LION
with a comb and a fork

We looked for things with teeth to paint with, and we found a comb and a fork. Can you think of anything else?

MATERIALS: *Combs, an old fork, paint, a brush, colored construction paper, a pencil, markers, scissors, a glue stick, and a plastic tray. Optional: zigzag scissors.*

1 Using the pencil, draw an animal that has fur, like a lion. Retrace the outline with a marker.

2 Get the paints that you want to use ready in the plastic tray. Dip the fork into the paint and paint the lion's mane. You can also color in the drawing with a brush and spread the color using the fork. But don't use the fork for eating after you've used it for this project!

16

3 Use the same technique for the background of your picture. The sun rays will look great if you dip the fork into the paint and lay it down flatter. For the grass, try using a comb.

4 Cut out the lion, and glue it onto the background you prepared by applying the glue stick on the reverse side of the lion.

Watch your friends and family's faces when they see that you can paint with anything you find in the house...

ANIMALS WITH SHELLS
with marbles

We're going to have a great race with these guys! You can also make a mobile with them and then, you can watch them while lying in bed.

MATERIALS: Colored construction papers, marbles, a cardboard box, a plate, scissors, glue stick, tape, a pen, and a marker.

1 Put the construction paper inside the cardboard box. There are two ways to paint: one is to put the paint on a plate, dip the marble into the paint and then put it in the box. The other way is to put a little paint directly on the construction paper, and then put the marble on it.

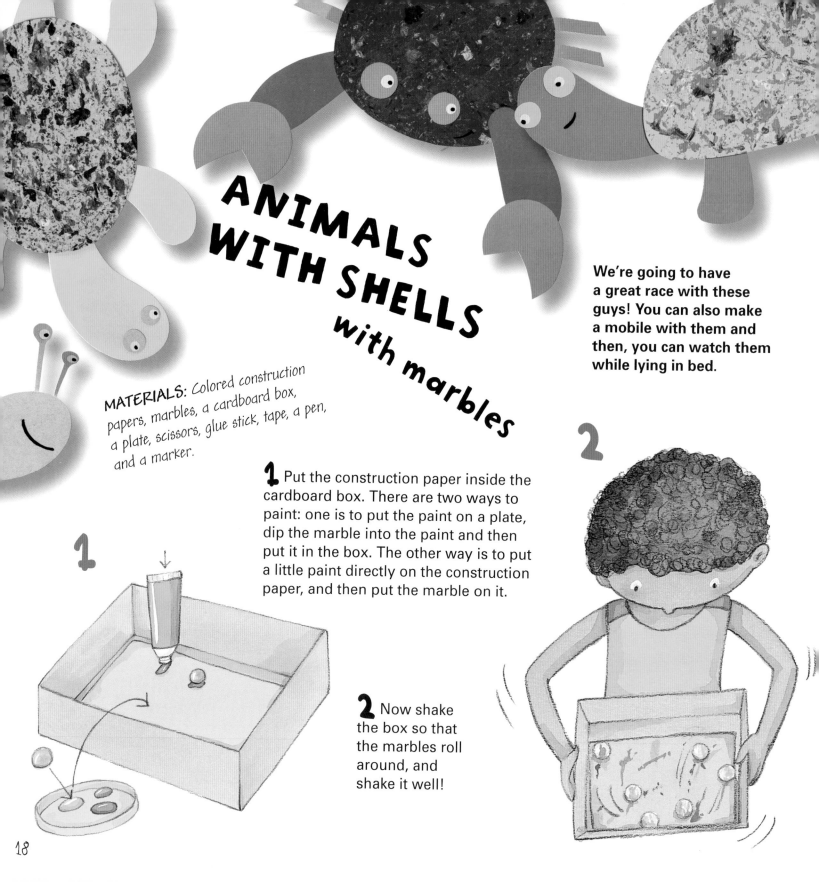

2 Now shake the box so that the marbles roll around, and shake it well!

3 You can repeat the process with different colored construction papers and paints. Once it's dry, cut out the shells of the animals you want to make.

4 To finish, draw and cut out the other parts of the animal's body. Glue them under the shell and use a little tape to make extra sure that they are secure and won't come off.

Now you know: marbles are a great game.... But they are also great for the fine arts too!

For your next birthday party, prepare some "professional" invitations. Take note!

MATERIALS: A plastic card (an expired credit card or something similar), colored construction papers, wooden frame, a piece of thin polyester fabric, tempera paint, acrylic paint, a paintbrush, a plastic sleeve, paper, and a pencil.

INVITATIONS
with a plastic card

1 Draw a simple picture in pencil on the paper. Put the plastic sleeve on the paper and trace the drawing with acrylic paint using the paintbrush. Now you have to use this paint to fill in all the areas where you DON'T want the colors to go. You're making a negative.

2 Before it dries, stick the plastic sleeve on the fabric. Make sure the paint soaks through well. Now remove the pencil drawing, and trace the painted areas with more paint and let it dry.

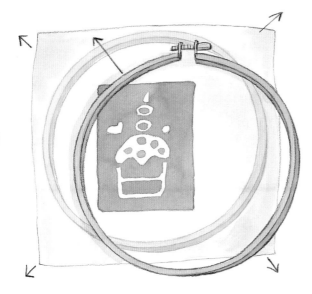

3 Once it dries, peel the fabric away from the plastic sleeve and stretch it in the wooden frame.

4 Get the construction paper ready and choose a tempera paint color. Put the construction paper underneath the fabric. Place a line of paint across the top of the fabric. Drag the paint down using the card, tilting it forward (see picture) and dragging it down. The paint will go through the fibers of the fabric onto the construction paper. Remove the construction paper carefully and let it dry. If you want to change colors, clean the fabric under running water and gently dry it.

What you have done looks a lot like a silk screen. It's a very useful technique for making a series of cards using the same design.

21

SEA LIFE PAINTINGS
with spray bottles

You will discover how to paint only the figures you want to using spray bottles.

MATERIALS: Spray bottles, white construction paper, removable self-adhesive paper, a pencil, scissors, dyes, newspaper, masking tape, and latex gloves. Optional: zigzag scissors, hole punch, and a piece of plastic.

1 Draw a basic silhouette on the back of the self-adhesive paper. Cut it out.

2 Remove the protective cover and stick the self-adhesive paper on the construction paper. Since you are going to work on this project from a standing position, protect the wall with newspaper and tape the construction paper to it.

3 Pour the dye you've picked into the spray bottle. If the color is too dark, add water.

4 Wear gloves to keep your hands clean and start spraying your drawing. You can make the color darker or lighter by spraying as much or as little as you like. Once it is dry, carefully remove the silhouette.

Cut a piece of plastic in zigzag and move it over the fish while you are spraying, and you will make the scales!

DOODLES with reeds

Doodles are those drawings that we do without thinking about them, the scribbling that we do when we're distracted.

MATERIALS: Thin reeds (preferably bamboo) or sticks like shish kebab sticks, black India ink, paper, coarse grain sandpaper. For older children: a box cutter, a fret saw, and an awl.

1

1 Sharpen the point of the reed or stick using the sandpaper on an angle, so that it has a diagonal slant.

2 The next step is dipping the stick in the ink… and let's paint! You'll have to keep dipping in the ink, and wipe the stick on the end of the bottle so it doesn't drip.

2

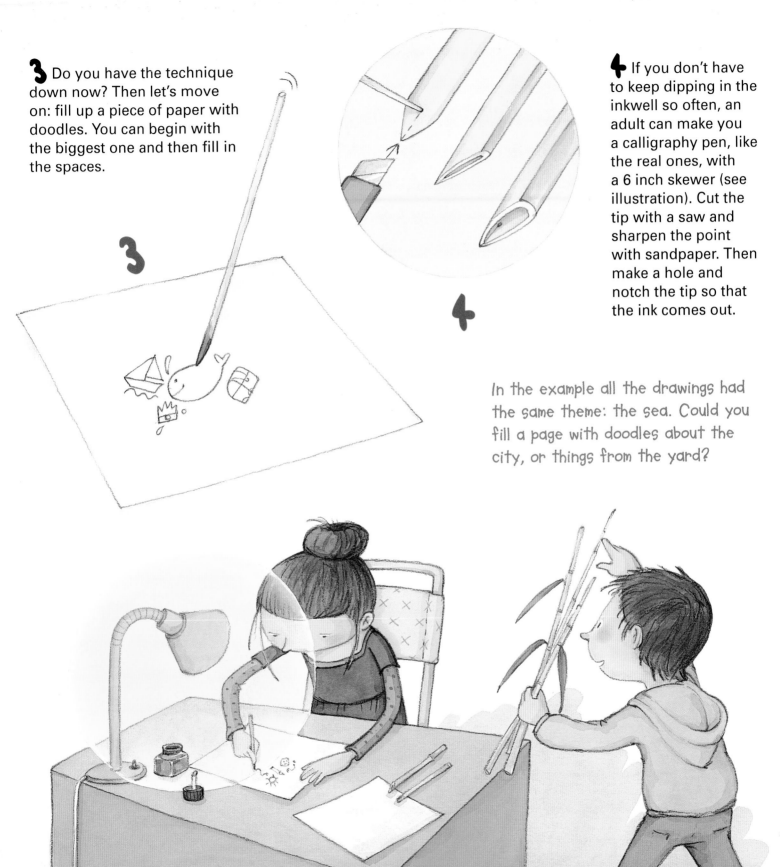

3 Do you have the technique down now? Then let's move on: fill up a piece of paper with doodles. You can begin with the biggest one and then fill in the spaces.

4 If you don't have to keep dipping in the inkwell so often, an adult can make you a calligraphy pen, like the real ones, with a 6 inch skewer (see illustration). Cut the tip with a saw and sharpen the point with sandpaper. Then make a hole and notch the tip so that the ink comes out.

In the example all the drawings had the same theme: the sea. Could you fill a page with doodles about the city, or things from the yard?

DECORATIVE LINES with bottles

Salt is white...
But it can also be lots
and lots of colors...

MATERIALS: Plastic bottles with one opening (like mustard or ketchup bottles, for example), salt, colored chalk, paper, and construction paper (or directly on the ground).

1

1 Pour a small pile of salt on the paper. Choose a piece of colored chalk and rub it against the salt to give it color.

2

2 Fold the paper in half and pour the salt into a bottle. Prepare several bottles using different colors.

3 And now you can try some borders, combine shapes and colors to make whatever you want. You can do it on the construction paper or directly on the ground.

4 When you're finished, clean up the colored sand. If it isn't dirty you can use the sand again next time.

It would also be fun to put paint into the bottles instead of sand, don't you think?

27

MANDALAS

Mandalas are always circular figures inside a square surface.

with cotton swabs

MATERIALS: *Cotton swabs, glossy colored art paper, scissors, a smooth paintbrush, acrylic paint, bowls for mixing paints. Optional: toothpicks.*

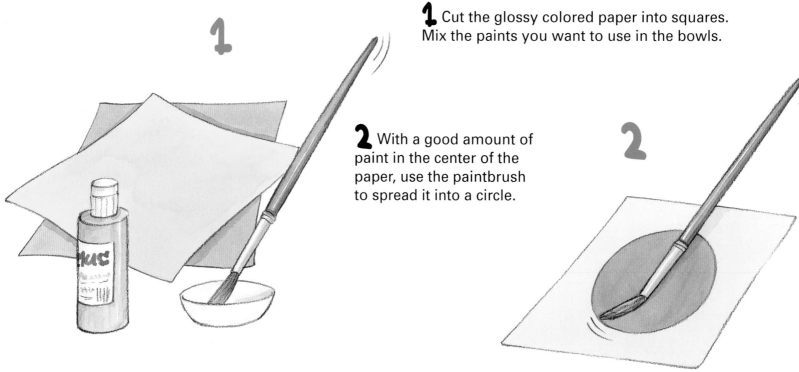

1 Cut the glossy colored paper into squares. Mix the paints you want to use in the bowls.

2 With a good amount of paint in the center of the paper, use the paintbrush to spread it into a circle.

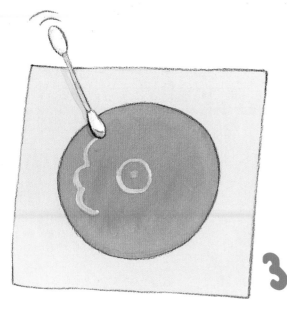

3 Immediately, draw in shapes using the cotton swab, pushing down to remove the paint before it dries. With every line you will see the color from the paper underneath come through.

3

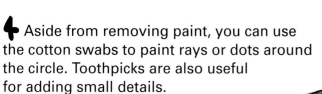

4

4 Aside from removing paint, you can use the cotton swabs to paint rays or dots around the circle. Toothpicks are also useful for adding small details.

You can do a lot of different combinations for the mandalas. Let your imagination run wild!

29

We are going to use the outlines of the beautiful things we find in nature to create new shapes using our imagination.

NATURE-THEMED CARDS
with a toothbrush

MATERIALS: *Toothbrushes, colored construction paper, paint, things from nature or household items (stones, leaves, wire, strings, spoons...), a plate, markers, and stickers.*

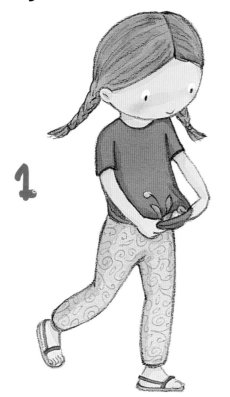

1 Find things that will help you make the shapes and figures you want: stones, leaves, a spoon.... Be creative...

2 Look at this butterfly: the body is a spoon, the wings are leaves, and the antenna are pieces of wire twisted into form. We put it all on a piece of construction paper. And the stones become...Ladybugs!

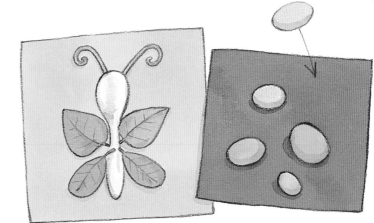

3 Once you've got your materials ready, pour some paint onto a plate and dip the toothbrush bristles in. Hold the toothbrush firmly and run your thumb over the bristles so that the paint splatters and leaves a dot pattern.

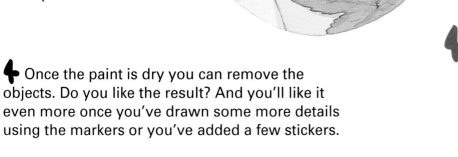

4 Once the paint is dry you can remove the objects. Do you like the result? And you'll like it even more once you've drawn some more details using the markers or you've added a few stickers.

Combining different shaped leaves can have some wonderful results!

OWLS
with glue bottles

Two owls, double up your good luck!

MATERIALS: White glue, black (or colored) acrylic paint, dye, watercolor paper (or construction paper or thick regular paper), a plate to mix paints, paintbrushes, a pencil, a glass of water, and tape.

1

1 Using a pencil, draw the figure you want on the construction paper. Just keep in mind that you have to have closed spaces so that you can fill it in later with different colors.

2 Next, pour the glue directly from the bottle and trace the whole drawing. Let it dry.

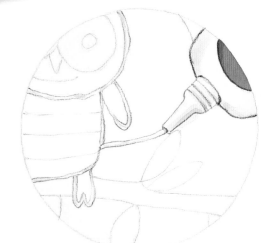

2

3 Put sticky tape around the edges of the paper (when you remove it, you'll be left with a white frame). Prepare the paint you need and … go for it! You don't have to be too careful, because the lines of glue will create a barrier so that you don't go over the lines. Paint each area a different color.

4 If you do it this way the borders will be clear. If you want the borders to be white, black, or colored, you just have to dye the glue with a little bit of paint before you go on to step two.

Did you notice that using this technique your painting looks like a stained glass window?

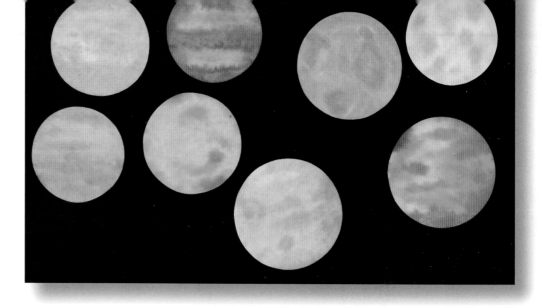

Do you like the planets and moons? Then you'll love this!

PLANET MOBILE

with an eye dropper

MATERIALS: *Eye droppers, coffee filters, dye, a compass, scissors, newspaper, something to mix the paints and dyes (a palette, or egg cartons, or ice-cube trays), glue stick, dark construction paper, reeds, or string.*

1 The first step is to draw circles on coffee filters using a compass. Draw a few and make them different sizes, then cut them out.

2 Look up the colors of the planets so that you can match the colors to the planets. Mix the paints.

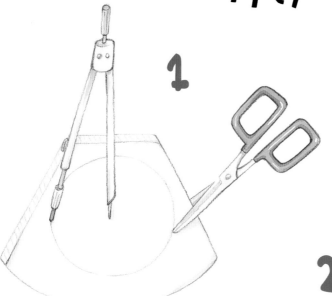

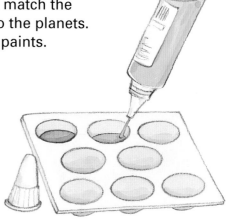

34

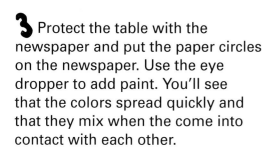

3 Protect the table with the newspaper and put the paper circles on the newspaper. Use the eye dropper to add paint. You'll see that the colors spread quickly and that they mix when the come into contact with each other.

4 Once they are dry, you can glue the circles to the dark construction paper so that they look like planets in the solar system.

The planets also look great hanging from a mobile in your room: run a string through the paper and tie them to a skewer or a stick.

First edition for North America published in 2015 by
Barron's Educational Series, Inc.
Original title of the book in Catalan: *L'art de pintar
sobre diferents objectes*
© Copyright GEMSER PUBLICATIONS S.L., 2015
c/Castell, 38; Teià(0829) Barcelona, Spain (World Rights)
Tel: 93 540 13 53
E-mail: *info@mercedesros.com*
Website: *www.mercedesros.com*
Author and illustrator: Bernadette Cuxart

ISBN: 978-1-4380-0653-6
Library of Congress Control No.: 2014949907

All inquiries should be addressed to:
Barron's Educational Series, Inc.
250 Wireless Boulevard
Hauppauge, NY 11788
www.barronseduc.com

Printed in China
9 8 7 6 5 4 3 2 1

Date of Manufacture: January 2015
Place of Manufacture: L. REX PRINTING COMPANY
    LIMITED, Dongguan City, Guangdong, China